KNITTING

KNITTING

PENNY HILL
SERIES EDITOR: ROSEMARY WILKINSON

SUNBURST BOOKS

ENGLISH KNITTING TERMS ARE USED THROUGHOUT

American terms which are different are as follows:

U.K.	U.S.
cast off	bind off
miss	skip
stocking stitch	stockinette stitch
tension	gauge
work straight	work even
yarn forward)	
yarn over needle)	yarn over
yarn round needle)	

Note: Imperial and metric measurements are not direct equivalents, so always follow only one set in a particular method.

This edition first published in 1994 by
Sunburst Books, Deacon House, 65 Old Church Street,
London SW3 5BS

Created and produced by
Rosemary Wilkinson and Malcolm Saunders Publishing Ltd
4 Lonsdale Square, London N1 1EN

ISBN 1 85778 044 2

Printed and bound in Hong Kong

Illustrations: Terry Evans
Design: Ming Cheung
Cover photograph: by courtesy of The Readicut Wool Co. Ltd.
Terry Mills, Ossett, West Yorkshire WF5 9SA

Contents

Introduction

Knitting needs no introduction, it is a long-established traditional craft that has been handed down from generation to generation. However, accepted skills, commonplace in our grandparents day, are now no longer learnt.

It is possible to teach yourself to knit and, with a little practice of the basic techniques shown in this book, you could become an expert in next to no time. This book guides you from the first steps of successful casting on through a host of favourite stitches; then explains how to translate the basic knowledge into specific features of knitted garments, such as hems and pockets. This handy-sized manual can be slipped into the knitting bag for quick and easy reference.

If you have never learnt to knit, now is the time to begin. It's a craft that's easy to do whether you are sitting at home or out, on a bus or a train, and will provide the key to a new wardrobe for you and your family.

Part 1:
EQUIPMENT

YARNS

Yarn is divided into two main types – natural and
synthetic. Natural yarn is more expensive, but is
more pleasant to wear and easier to handle when
knitting. Synthetic yarn is cheaper but stronger and
lasts longer.

NATURAL YARNS

Wool which is easily available, long lasting and very
warm comes from sheep which are bred for their
fleeces. Merino sheep have the most abundant and
highest quality yarn.

Mohair yarn comes from goats which originated in
Turkey. The long brushed fibres are extremely
thick and warm.

Angora is an expensive soft and warm yarn which
comes from the short haired albino rabbit of the
same name.

Chenille is a yarn with many short hairs, rather like
velvet.

Cashmere, the most expensive and luxurious of
yarns, is spun with a high percentage of wool and
comes from a special breed of goat.

Alpaca is a soft, high quality fibre with a slight
hairiness which comes from a species of camel.

Silk knitting yarns are heavy and therefore
expensive, but mixed with other fibres produce a
strong, durable thread.

Cotton is a strong, non allergenic, easy to wash and wear yarn that has little elasticity.

Linen comes from the flax plant, is stronger than cotton and is usually blended with wool for more elasticity.

SYNTHETIC YARNS

Man-made yarns have improved dramatically over the last few years; these yarns are no longer lifeless with little elasticity. With clever combinations of synthetic and natural fibres, fashionable, strong and lightweight yarns can be produced. Their cost compares favourably with the more expensive natural fibres.

Lurex is a shining metallic yarn available in many colours, or a single thread may be used as one of the plys when the yarn is spun.

THE THICKNESS OF YARN

Yarn is formed by twisting together a number of strands, or plys, of fibre. The terms 3-ply, 4-ply, double knitting, Aran and Chunky are only general descriptions for yarns as plys can vary in thickness, so great care has to be taken when substituting yarns. Always check that the substitute yarn produces the correct tension (see page 37).

THE TEXTURE OF YARN

During the spinning process the fibres can be fused together at different rates. **Bouclé** is produced by introducing one ply at a faster rate than the other two, so that it buckles up. **Mohair** is a brushed loop yarn, giving it a fluffy appearance. **Slub yarns** have at least one ply that varies in thickness producing an uneven look. **Tweed effects** are formed by adding coloured blips to longer fibres.

READING A BALL–BAND

The printed band round a ball of wool gives various pieces of useful information on laundering the yarn, which needles are suitable and sometimes which crochet hook is suggested.

The information is given graphically through symbols but also with brief explanatory text. Below are the most common international symbols used:

The suggested appropriate needle size for the particular wool. A knitting pattern will also stipulate a needle size for working the pattern. If this is different from the manufacturer's recommendation, follow the size given in the pattern, as this will have been used to produce the specific tension for the pattern.

The suggested appropriate crochet hook size for the particular wool. See note above.

Hand wash only.

 Machine washable at stated temperature and stated wash program. Temperatures for cottons are shown without a bar underneath the symbol; for synthetics with a single bar and for wools with a broken bar.

 May be bleached (with chlorine).

 May be tumble dried. Where dots appear in the symbol, two dots means a high heat setting; one dot a low heat setting.

 Iron with cool iron.

Iron with warm iron.

 Iron with hot iron.

 May be dry cleaned - the letter within the circle indicates which solutions may be used. Show the label to your dry cleaner.

 A cross through any symbol means DO NOT.

NEEDLES AND RELATED ITEMS

All that is needed to produce a piece of knitted fabric is a pair of knitting needles, although you may find some other items rather useful.
Needles are available in plastic, wood, bamboo, steel or alloy. Whichever one you choose, it should make no difference to the tension or quality of your work. It is all a matter of personal preference.

Most types of knitting are worked with pairs of needles but some garments are worked in rounds requiring circular or double-pointed needles and some patterns, such as cable, use special needles in conjunction with the pairs of needles.

Pairs of needles These range in size from 0 to 15 US sizes, 2mm to 10mm metric sizes and come in three lengths 10in(25cm), 12in(30cm) and 14in(35cm) - use the length which you find comfortable for the number of stitches you are working with and the type of pattern you are knitting.

THE CHART BELOW GIVES U.S. AND METRIC CONVERSIONS AS WELL AS THE OLD ENGLISH SYSTEM OF GRADING NEEDLES.

KNITTING NEEDLES

U.S.	Metric	U.K.
0	2mm	14
1	2 1/4mm	13
	2 1/2mm	
2	2 3/4mm	12
	3mm	11
3	3 1/4mm	10
4	3 1/2mm	
5	3 3/4mm	9
	4mm	8
6		
7	4 1/2mm	7
8	5mm	6
9	5 1/2mm	5
10	6mm	4
10 1/2	6 1/2mm	3
	7mm	2
	7 1/2mm	1
11	8mm	0
13	9mm	00
15	10mm	00

Circular needles are used for knitting tubular, seamless fabric or for knitting flat rounds. Circular needles are two short metal needles joined by a length of nylon. They can also be used as a pair of needles, working backwards and forwards, if working a large number of stitches.
Keep the needles in their packet as they do not have their size stamped on them.

Double-pointed needles are available in sets of four or six. They are used for knitting seamless socks, gloves and berets.They are also often used to knit neckbands and can be used as an alternative to a circular needle where there is a small number of stitches which may be too stretched on a circular needle.

Cable needles are short, straight - or they may have a U-bend - needles which come in three sizes. They are used for moving stitches from one position to another when working cables. Use the needle which corresponds to the yarn and main needles.

Stitch-holders are useful for "holding" a small amount of stitches until they are needed. Safety pins can be used for four or five stitches.

Needle gauge is useful for checking sizes of circular and double-pointed needles which do not have the size on them.

Yarn bobbins are used for small amounts of yarn, wound from the main ball, when working colour patterns.

Row counters are helpful for keeping track of the number of rows. They are small cylinders which slip onto the end of the needle. You wind on the figures at the end of each row.

ANCILLARY EQUIPMENT

Tape measure - choose a strong measure that cannot stretch as this can distort your measurements. Always use either inches or centimetres, rather than a mixture of the two.

Scissors can be small but must be sharp as some yarns are very strong and cannot be broken.

Pins can disappear in the knitting if they are too small, so choose long ones with coloured glass heads.

Sewing needles with large eyes and blunt ends are used for sewing up - sharp needles can split the yarn and weaken it.

Crochet hooks - a small, medium and large size are useful for picking up dropped stitches and working edgings on finished garments.

Corks are used to put on the pointed end of knitting needles to prevent stitches from falling off and to make them safer when not in use. There are also commercial gadgets available for the same purpose.

Teasel brushes are used to brush mohair and restore the fluffiness when it has been knitted.

Markers are small plastic loops that can be clipped onto a stitch for easier recognition later.

Chart magnifiers are long, clear plastic, semi-circular tubes, the flat side sits on the chart and magnifies the symbols, making them easier to read.

Part 2:
TECHNIQUES

Before You Begin

Before casting on, get used to holding the needle and yarn, this is very important as it controls the tension of the finished fabric.

There are many ways of casting on, but the English method is the one most commonly used. The instructions given are for right-handed knitters.

Left-handed Knitters

Knitting right-handed can be confusing for left-handed people. To follow the instructions for casting on prop the book in front of a mirror and follow the diagrams in the mirror image. The yarn will then be controlled by the left hand. Knitting by the continental method (see page 27) may be the solution, as you are working in the same direction as a right-handed knitter, but holding the yarn in the left hand.

Holding the Yarn

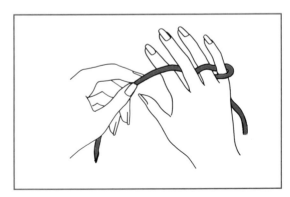

Hold the yarn in the left hand, pass it under the little finger of the other hand, then around the same finger, over the third finger, under the second finger and over the index finger, leaving enough to make the initial slip knot to cast on.

The index finger of the right hand is used to wind the yarn around the tip of the needle. The yarn wound around the little finger controls the tension of the yarn.

HOLDING THE NEEDLES

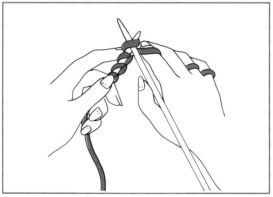

Hold the right needle in the same position as a pencil. For casting on and the first few rows the knitting passes between the thumb and index finger. As the knitting grows, place the thumb under the knitting, holding the needle from below.

Hold the left needle lightly over the top using the thumb to hold the stitches about to be worked and index finger to control the tip.

CASTING ON

This method of casting on gives a neat, firm edge with a cable appearance.

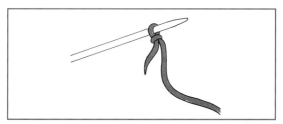

1 Make a slip knot near the end of the yarn and place it on the lefthand needle.

2 Holding the yarn at the back of the needles, insert the tip of the righthand needle into the loop, pass the yarn around the tip of the right needle.

3 Draw the righthand needle through the slip knot, forming a loop on the righthand needle, leave the slip knot on the lefthand needle.

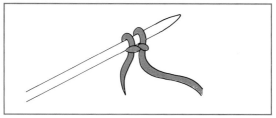

4 Transfer the new loop on to the lefthand needle, twisting it as you do so. There are now two stitches on the lefthand needle.

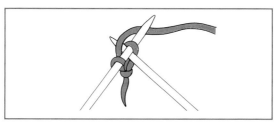

5 Insert the righthand needle between the two stitches on the lefthand needle, wind the yarn around the point of the righthand needle.

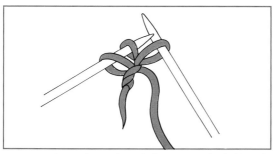

6 Draw a loop through and place it on the lefthand needle.
Repeat steps 5 and 6 until you have the required number of stitches.

BASIC STITCHES

All knitting stitches, even the most complicated, are made from either knitting or purling.

How to knit

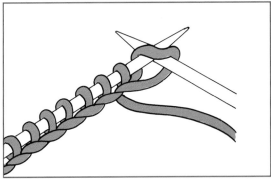

1 Hold the needle with the cast-on stitches in your left hand. With the yarn at the back of the work insert the right needle, from front to back through the first stitch on the lefthand needle.

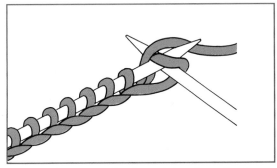

2 Wind the yarn under the righthand needle, then from left to right over the top.

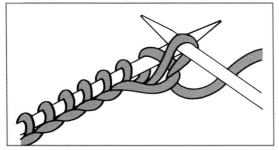

3 Draw the yarn through the stitch on the lefthand needle, making a new stitch on the righthand needle.

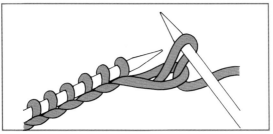

4 Slip the original stitch off the lefthand needle.

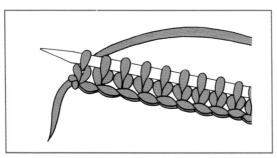

To knit a row, repeat steps 1 to 4 until all the stitches have been transferred from the left needle to the right needle.

Turn the work and transfer the needle containing
the stitches to the left hand in order to work the
next row.

How to purl

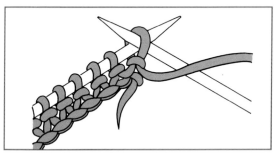

1 Hold the needle with the stitches on in your left
hand. With the yarn at the front of the work insert
the right needle, through the front of the first stitch
on the lefthand needle.

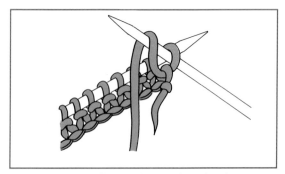

2 Wind the yarn from right to left under the point
of the righthand needle.

3 Draw the yarn through the stitch on the lefthand

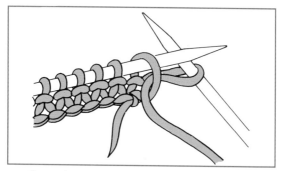

needle, making a new stitch on the righthand needle.

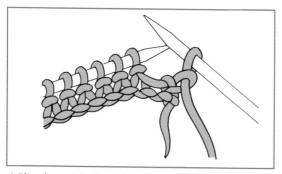

4 Slip the original stitch off the lefthand needle.

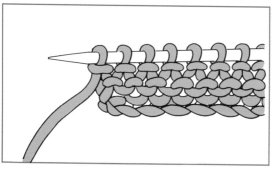

To purl a row, repeat steps 1 to 4 until all the

stitches have been transferred from the left needle to the right needle.

Turn the work and transfer the needle containing the stitches to the left hand in order to work the next row.

How to cast off

Casting off should be done in the same stitch at the same tension as the knitting, if it is too tight it will pucker. If this happens, try using a larger needle. It is less likely that the casting off will be too slack, but if it is, try a smaller needle.

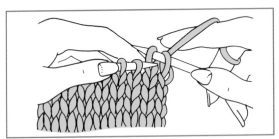

1 Knit the first two stitches in the usual way, so both the stitches are on the righthand needle.

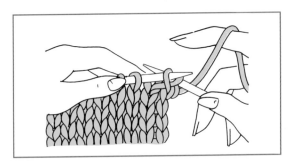

2 Use the point of the lefthand needle to lift the first knitted stitch over the second stitch and off the needle.

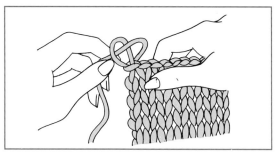

3 Knit another stitch onto the righthand needle, repeat from step 2 until one stitch remains. Leaving a long length for seaming, lengthen the stitch, remove the needle, then pull the end through the stitch to tighten it.

How to knit – continental style

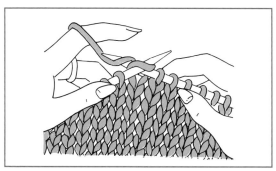

1 Hold the yarn in your left hand with it looped round the index finger. Insert the righthand needle from front to back into the stitch to be knitted, then twist it under the working strand of yarn from index finger.

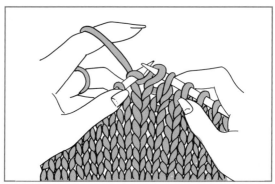

2 Use the righthand needle to draw through a new stitch, then drop the original stitch from the left-hand needle.

How to purl – continental style

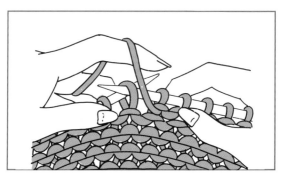

1 Holding the yarn in your left hand and keeping your index finger to the right of where you are working, insert the righthand needle from back to front through the stitch to be purled.

2 Bring the working yarn forward slightly, then twist the righthand needle from left to right around the yarn. Use the righthand needle to draw through a new stitch, then drop the original stitch from the lefthand needle.

JOINING IN A NEW BALL OF YARN

Unless an enormous ball of yarn is used, it will be necessary at some time or other to join in a new ball of yarn. Try to do this at the end of a row, as it is difficult to darn in an end in the middle of a row neatly.

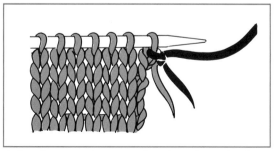

1 Leaving enough yarn to darn in, using a simple knot, join the new yarn to the first stitch.

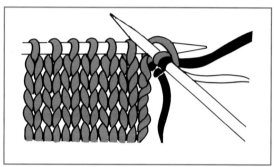

2 Secure the join by working the first stitch with two ends of yarn, one from the new ball and the tail end of the old yarn, then continue the row with the new colour only.

INCREASING

Adding stitches, by one of a number of methods, is used to shape the fabric, making it wider.

Knitting into the same stitch twice

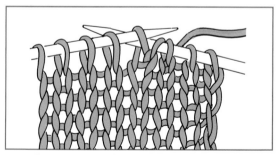

On a knit row, knit first into the front of the stitch then, without dropping the original stitch, knit also into the back of the stitch, thus making two stitches from one.

On a purl row, purl first into the front of the stitch then into the back of the stitch.

Invisible increasing

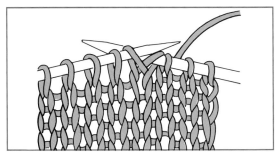

Before working the stitch on the needle, knit into the stitch below the one on the needle, then into the stitch on the needle. This method can also be used on a purl row.

Raised increasing

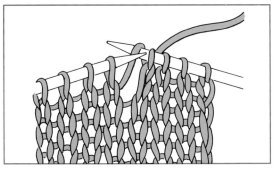

Using the righthand needle, pick up the bar that lies between the stitch just worked on the righthand needle and the next stitch on the lefthand needle.

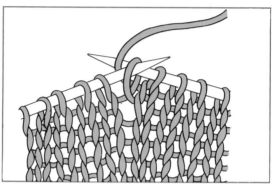

Place the bar on the left needle, twisting it as you do and knit into the back of it.

Making a stitch between two knit stitches

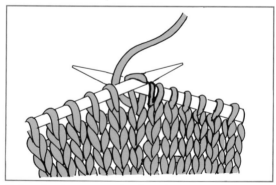

Bring the the yarn to the front between the needles, then take over the right needle before knitting the next stitch. This is described as "yarn forward" (abbreviated to "yf") in a knitting pattern.

Making a stitch between two purl stitches

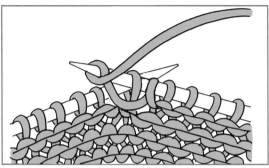

Take yarn over the right needle to the back of the work, then bring the yarn to the front between the needles. This is described as "yarn round needle" (abbreviated to "yrn") in a knitting pattern.

Making a stitch between a knit and a purl stitch

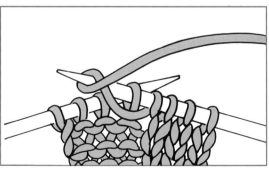

Having worked a knit stitch, bring the yarn forward under the righthand needle, then wind it over the needle and back to the front, purl the next stitch.

Extending a row

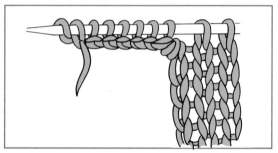

Cast on the required number of stitches at the beginning or end of the row, using the usual method.

DECREASING

Decreasing, by any one of a number of methods, is used to reduce the number of stitches, making the fabric narrower.

Basic decreasing

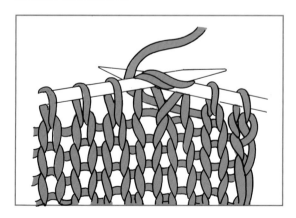

This is the simplest and most commonly used method. Insert the righthand needle from left to right through the second then the first stitch on left-hand needle, knit the two stitches together, making one. This is described as "knit 2 together" (k2tog) in a knitting pattern.

Purl decreasing

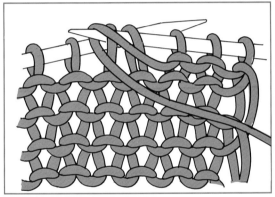

Insert the righthand needle from right to left through the first two stitches on the lefthand needle, purl the two stitches together, making one stitch. This is described as "purl 2 together" (p2tog) in a knitting pattern.

Slip stitch decreasing

Slip a stitch from the lefthand needle onto the righthand needle, knit the next stitch then, using the tip of the left needle, pass the slipped stitch over the last stitch on right needle (as shown overleaf). This is described as "slip 1, knit 1, pass slipped stitch

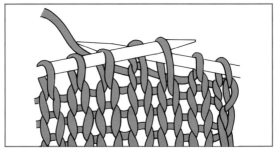

over" (sl1, k1, psso) in a knitting pattern.

Following a pattern

Most knitting patterns are produced by yarn manu-
facturers or appear in magazines. They give you all
the information you need to produce a garment that
looks like the illustration. The information is usually
presented in a logical form that is easy to follow.

Materials are usually listed in the first paragraph
that appears on the pattern. The list details how
much yarn you need, what size needles to use and
whether you need cable needle or buttons, etc.

Measurements are very important as they tell you
what the finished size of the garment will be.
Compare the actual measurements with the "to fit"
measurements as the amount of ease given can vary
from style to style. You may want to make a size
smaller or larger than the size to fit you, if you do
not feel happy will the amount of room in the
garment.

As a rough guide, the relation between your body
measurement and the fit of a knitted garment is as
follows:

> very close fitting / body hugging – 2in (5cm) less than your bust size
>
> close fitting / contoured against body – up to 1in (3cm) more than bust size
>
> standard fitting / body-skimming – 2in (5cm) more than bust size
>
> loose fitting / hangs against body – 4in (10cm) more than bust
>
> oversized / very roomy – 5in (13cm) or more than bust size

A pattern will usually be written to suit three or four different sizes. Any variation in the number of stitches required will be given in brackets, e.g. an instruction might read: "to suit sizes 10 (12, 14) cast on 30 (40, 50) stitches". Once you have decided which size is for you, go through the pattern and mark all the instructions related to your size so that it is easy to read.

Tension is the most important part of producing a perfect garment. The tension stated in the pattern is the one obtained by the designer, using the quoted yarn and needle size, and therefore used to design the garment and produce the stated measurements.

Making and measuring a tension swatch

To check that your tension matches the one given in the instructions, make a sample swatch, using the yarn, needles and stitch stated in the pattern. The tension is usually given over 4in(10cm), but make a swatch at least 6in(15cm) square. Place the sample on a padded surface and gently smooth it into shape without distorting the stitches. Pin the

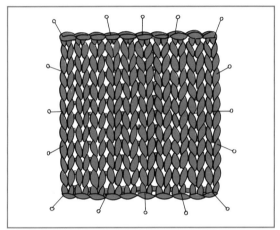

corners and sides as shown, unrolling the edges if necessary and inserting the pins at right angles to the fabric. The tension of both the stitches across the rows and the rows themselves needs to be checked.

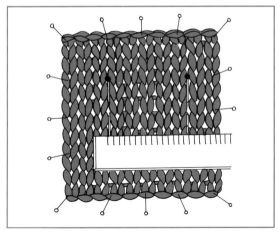

For the stitch tension, use pins as markers and count the number of stitches recommended in the tension given. Using a rigid ruler measure the distance between the pins. If your tension is correct it should measure 4in(10cm). If you have fewer stitches than stated it means your knitting is too loose, if you have more stitches than stated your knitting is too tight. If your tension is too loose make another swatch using one size smaller needles. If your tension is too tight make another swatch using larger needles.

It is well worth spending the time before you start on the actual pattern to get it right. Your tension must be accurate, if it is only one stitch out, it could make the finished garment too big or too small.

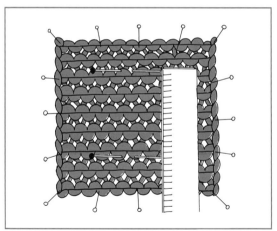

For the row tension, follow the same procedure as for the stitch tension. On stocking stitch, it may be easier work from the back as each ridge is one row. If your stitch tension is accurate but your row tension is slightly out, this should not make much difference to most garments.

Abbreviations

These are used in knitting patterns to keep the instructions short and precise. If every word was written in long hand, each pattern would make a small book. The following abbreviations are the ones most commonly used:

alt - alternate
approx - approximately
beg - beginning
cm - centimetres
CN - cable needle
cont - continue
C4B - cable 4 back, slip next 2 sts onto CN and hold at back of work, k2, then k2 from CN
C4F - cable 4 front, slip next 2 sts onto CN and hold at front of work, k2, then k2 from CN
Cr3L - cross 3 front, slip next 2 sts onto CN and hold at front of work, p1, then k2 from CN
Cr3R - cross 3 back, slip next st onto CN and hold at back of work, k2, then p1 from CN
dec - decrease(ing)
dpn - double-pointed needles
foll - following
g-st - garter st, every row k
in - inches
inc - increase(ing)
k - knit
LH - lefthand
m1 - make one st by picking up the bar between the st just worked and the next st on lefthand needle and working into the back of it
MB - make bobble, (exact instructions will be given for the type and size of bobble used)
mm - millimetres

p - purl
patt - pattern
psso - pass slipped stitch over
rem - remain(ing)
rep - repeat
RH - righthand
RS - right side
sl - slip
st(s) - stitch(es)
st st - stocking stitch, k on right side and p back
tbl - through back of loop
tog - together
WS - wrong side
ytf - yarn to front
yf - yarn forward to make one st

Written instructions

The main part of the pattern contains written instructions which tell you how to make a garment from beginning to end. The instructions are given headings which are usually in a bold type so they are easily spotted when reading the instructions. An asterisk (★) is a common symbol in knitting instructions. It is used to save the same instruction being used over and over again, for example, ★ p1, k1; rep from ★ to end of row means you just keep working p1, k1, until the last stitch has been knitted. Another space saving technique is to put instructions that are to repeated in square brackets [ ] and then state how many times they are to be repeated, for example [p1, k1] 4 times.

There are other commonly used terms with specific meanings as follows:

cast off in rib - when casting off, keep to the rib pattern, i.e. cast off the knit stitches with a knit stitch and the purl with a purl.

knitwise - insert the needle into the stitch as if you were going to knit a stitch.

pick up and knit (purl) - pick up the stitches with a knit (purl) stitch.

purlwise - insert the needle into the stitch as if you were going to purl a stitch.

work straight - continue working the pattern without any increasing or decreasing.

Measuring your work is a most important part of producing a well fitting garment. Lay the piece of knitting on a flat surface, if necessary knit to the middle of the row so that the stitches are not all bunched up on the needle. Using a rigid ruler, take all measurements on the straight, never measure round curves.

Making up the garment should be done with great care. The knitted pieces may need to be pressed first, as described below, before sewing up following one of the methods on pages 43 - 46. A beautifully knitted garment can be spoilt by bad making up. It cannot be rushed.

Blocking is the term used for pinning and pressing. Prepare a padded surface - a blanket on a table and covered with a clean cloth will suffice. Lay the knitted piece, wrong side up and smooth it out to the correct measurements. Check that the rows and edges are running straight. Place pins through the knitted edge at right angles to it, at frequent inter-vals to obtain a smooth line. Do not pin or press any rib sections, as this would affect their elasticity.

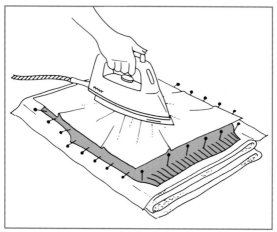

Follow the pressing instructions on the ball-band (see pages 11 and 12), using a pressing cloth, wet or dry, place over the knitting and with the iron set at the correct temperature, move the iron from section to section by lifting it up and placing it down. Do not use an ironing movement as this could distort the stitches. Leave the knitting to dry completely before removing the pins.

SEWING UP

This can be done using a variety of stitches, depending on what sort of edges are to be sewn together. Generally, you should use the same yarn for making up that the garment was knitted with. For thick yarns it may be possible to split the yarn to make thinner strands. For a textured yarn, use a matching smooth yarn.

Backstitch seams are strong and give a firm seam, they are mainly used on cast-off edges and uneven seams.

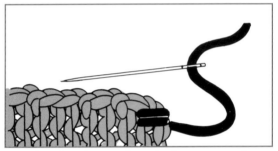

1 With right sides together, pin the seam together. Make a double stitch to begin with.

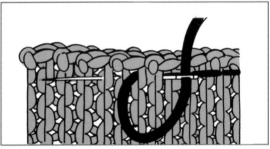

2 Make a running stitch no more than ³/₈in(1cm) long and push the needle through the fabric from the back to the front, pull the thread through. Take a backward stitch, inserting the needle at the end of the last stitch, bring the needle through the fabric from back to front a further ³/₈in(1cm) on. Pull the thread through. Continue in this way to the end of the seam. Finish with a double stitch. Do not pull up the stitches too tightly, otherwise there will be no "give" or elasticity in the seams.

Overcast seams are used for heavy yarns, sewing on front bands and collars.

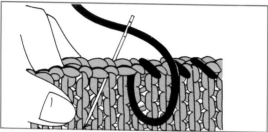

1 On stocking stitch fabric, with right sides together and edges aligned, match row ends. Work with the index finger between the fabrics. Join on the yarn and use the knots at the edges of the pieces as a guide to stitch length. Insert the needle behind the knot of the edge of the back piece, then through the corresponding knot on the other piece, pull the yarn through. Continue in this way to the end of the seam.

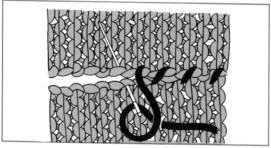

2 For a garter stitch fabric, lay the pieces side by side, wrong sides uppermost. Thread the needle through the bottom of the stitch on one side and the top of the corresponding stitch on the other side. This produces a flat seam which does not interrupt the lines of garter stitch.

Invisible seaming is the method knitters use for a professional finish. This seam is most suitable for straight stocking stitch edges. You work from the front, so you can see exactly what you are doing.

1 With right sides of both pieces of fabric facing upwards, join in the yarn, and thread the needle under the horizontal strand linking the edge stitch and the next stitch, pass the needle under two rows, then bring it to the front.

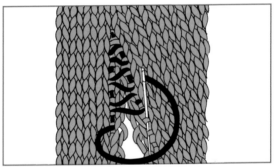

2 Return to the opposite side and working under two rows at a time throughout, repeat this zig-zag action always taking the needle under two rows and insert the needle into the hole that the last stitch on that side came out of. When the thread is pulled up the seam becomes invisible.

PICKING UP STITCHES

Once the main body of the knitting is compete it is often necessary to pick up stitches to work a border, this can be a neckband, collar, front edging, cuffs or armbands. The technique of picking up stitches along an edge is referred to as "pick up and knit" as stitches are made with new yarn rather than the loops of the main fabric.

When working from a pattern you will be told how many stitches to pick up. Great care must be taken to ensure that the stitches are picked up evenly along the edge: using pins divide the edge into eighths, divide the stitches required by eight and pick up this number of stitches in each section, checking the total number of stitches at the end.

Working along a cast-on or cast-off edge

With right side facing and holding a needle in your right hand, insert the point from front to back under both loops of the cast-on or cast-off edge, starting at the righthand edge of the piece. Wind the yarn round the needle as though knitting a stitch and draw a loop through forming a stitch on the needle. Continue in this way until the required number of stitches are picked up.

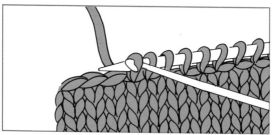

A crochet hook can be used to pull the loops through the edge and onto the needle.

Working along a side edge

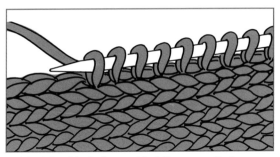

With right side facing and holding a needle in your right hand, insert the point from front to back between the first and second stitch in from the edge, wind the yarn around the needle as though knitting a stitch and draw a loop through forming a stitch on the needle. Continue in this way until the required number of stitches are picked up.

GRAFTING

This is a method of invisibly joining two sections of knitting using a blunt-ended needle. It works best from the right side on stocking stitch.

1 Lay the two pieces of knitting on a flat surface with the needles together, facing the same direction. Slip 2 or 3 stitches off both needles at a time. Using the same thread as the knitting, secure it at the back of the work and insert the needle from back to front through the first lower loop.

2 Thread the needle from front to back through the first upper loop then from back to front through the next upper loop. Insert the needle from front to

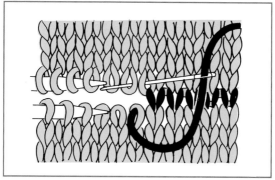

back through the first lower loop, then from front
to back through the next lower loop. Continue in
this way, slipping a few stitches off the needles at a
time and making sure that you always work twice
through each loop.

STRIPES

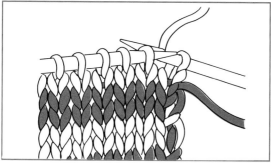

When working stripes up to 1in (3cm) wide with
an even number of rows, there is no need to cut off
and join in new yarns at every colour change.
Simply carry the unused wool up the side of the
work until you need it.

Part 3:
PATTERNS

BASIC FABRICS

All knitted fabrics are made using just two basic stitches, knit and purl.

Garter stitch

Garter stitch is often referred to as plain knitting because every row is worked in the same stitch, which can be either knit or purl. This produces a reversible fabric with raised horizontal ridges on both sides of the work. It is looser than stocking stitch. One of the advantages of garter stitch is that it does not curl so it can be used on its own, or for bands and borders.

Stocking stitch

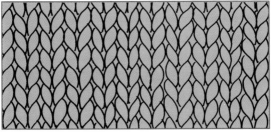

This is the most widely used knitted fabric. With the knit side as the right side it makes a flat, smooth surface that tends to curl at the edges. It needs finishing with bands, borders or hems where there would otherwise be a raw edge. The reverse side looks similar to garter stitch.

Single rib

A single rib is formed by alternating knit and purl stitches to form columns of stitches. It produces a very elastic fabric, ideal for welts, neckbands and borders. It is generally knitted on a smaller needle than the main fabric to keep it firm and elastic.

For an even number of stitches the pattern will be as follows.

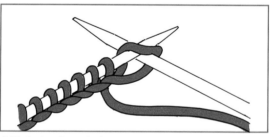

1 Knit the first stitch.

2 Bring the yarn through the needles to the front of the work and purl the next stitch.

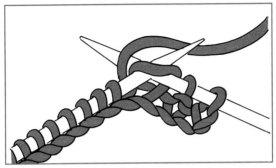

3 Take the yarn through the needles to the back of the work and knit the next stitch.

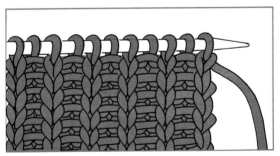

Repeat steps 2 and 3 until all the stitches are on the right needle, ending with a purl stitch.

Turn the work and start again from step 1.

For an odd number of stitches, the first stitch of each row will alternate between knit and purl.

Moss stitch

This is a basic textured stitch. It is made up of alternating knit and purl stitches, that is, stitches that are knitted on one row, will be knitted on the next

row and stitches that are purled on one row will be purled on the following row. If an odd number of stitches are cast on, every row will begin and end with a knit stitch. The fabric is firm, non curling and reversible, making it an ideal stitch for collars and cuffs.

For an odd number of stitches, the instructions will read:
Patt row: K1, ★ p1, k1; rep from ★ to end.
Repeat this row.

FAIR ISLE KNITTING

Fair Isle patterns can be given either as written instructions, which are very long when written out row by row, or as a chart.

Working from a chart

The chart is drawn on graph paper with a different symbol being used for each colour which makes the pattern easy to visualise at a glance.

Rows: When reading the chart, odd numbered rows, which are knit rows, are read from right to left, even numbered rows, which are purl rows, are read from left to right.

Stitches: Usually only one repeat of the pattern is given in the chart, the stitches which form the repeat are usually indicated by the words "rep these sts". Any stitches that will not divide into the pattern are charted either side of the pattern repeat and are knitted at the beginning and ends of the rows to balance the pattern.

Working with two colours

When working with two colours it is important to keep the tension correct. To do this you have to strand the yarn not being used across the back of the work over no more than five stitches. Alternatively, the yarn not being used can be woven into the yarn being knitted.

Whichever method is used, the work must remain elastic and the stitches even.

Holding the yarns

Working with two colours sounds difficult but with a little practice you can soon develop your own rhythm and keep the tension even.

Use one colour in each hand, the main in your right hand and the contrast in your left hand, with

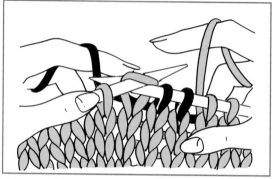

the yarn held across each index finger, ready for use. This method keeps the yarns from tangling, which can be a problem with stranded knitting.

Stranding

The colour not in use is carried loosely across the back of the work until it is required, but do not work more than five stitches in one colour. The fabric should look as neat on the back as it does on the front, with the strands loose and untwisted, one colour is always on the top and the other below it.

Stranding on a knit row

Hold the main colour in your right hand and the contrast in your left hand. Work as normal with the right hand and main colour, carrying the contrast colour loosely across the wrong side of the work.

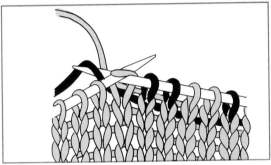

When the contrast colour is required, insert the righthand needle into the next stitch and draw a loop through from the yarn held in the left hand, carrying the main yarn loosely across the back of the work.

Stranding on a purl row

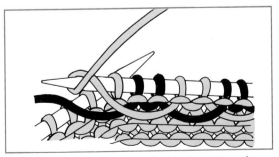

On a purl row, work as usual with the main colour,

holding the contrast colour in your left hand.

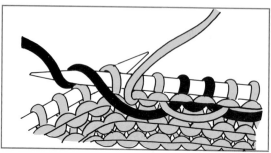

To purl a stitch in contrast colour, insert the right-hand needle into the next stitch and draw a loop through.

Weaving

Weaving is a method of looping the colour not in use around the colour being used on every other stitch.

Weaving on a knit row

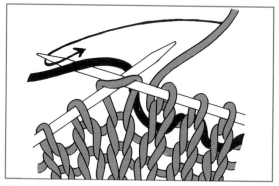

To weave in the contrast colour, held in the left

hand, knit the first stitch in the usual way, then on the second and every alternate stitch, insert the righthand needle into the stitch, then bring the contrast colour over the needle tip from right to left. Knit the stitch as usual, drawing the main colour under the contrast colour to pull it through the stitch.

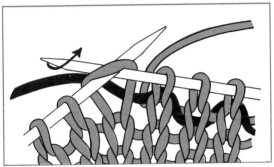

Knit the next stitch with the contrast colour under the right needle.

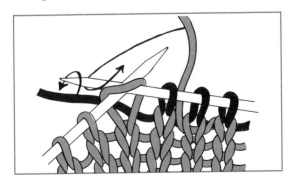

To weave in the main colour, held in the right hand, insert the righthand needle into the next

stitch, then wind the main colour knitwise around
the needle. Wind the contrast yarn around the
needle tip from left to right.

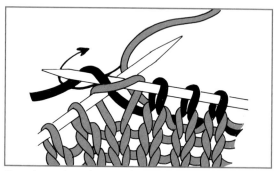

Pass the main colour in front of the contrast and
back under the right needle tip, hold it in this
position as the contrast yarn is drawn through to
form a new stitch.

Weaving on a purl row

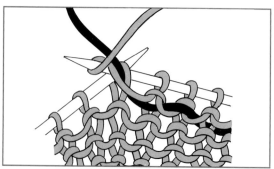

To weave in the contrast colour, held in the left
hand, on a purl row, purl the first stitch in the usual
way, then to work the second and every alternate

stitch, insert the righthand needle into the stitch, and bring the contrast colour over the needle tip. Purl the stitch as usual, drawing the main colour under the contrast colour to pull it through the stitch.

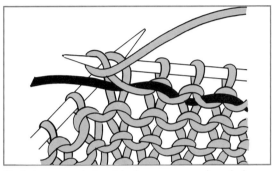

Purl the next stitch with the contrast colour below the needle.

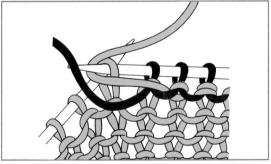

To weave in the main colour, held in the right hand, on a purl row, insert the righthand needle into the next stitch. Wind the main colour under the right needle tip to the back, then position the contrast colour over the needle tip from front to back, ready to purl the stitch.

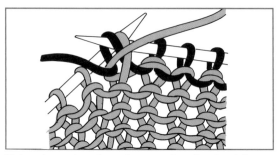

Bring the main colour down and under the right
needle tip over the contrast colour to the front.
The contrast colour can now easily be drawn
through to complete the stitch.

ARAN KNITTING

Aran jumpers are knitted in one colour as flat pieces.

Nearly all Aran patterns are formed by either
cabling or twisting stitches. However difficult a
pattern may look, the basic techniques still apply to
create the diamonds, lattices and many other pattern
variations.

Cables

Cables are vertical patterns, so called because they
look like twisted ropes. The cable will twist either
to the right or to the left, depending on whether
the slipped stitches are left at the back or the front
of the work.

Cables are usually worked in a stocking stitch
column on a reversed stocking stitch background.
They can be worked over any number of even

stitches. The more stitches in the cable, the more rows that are worked between the cable twists.

How to make a Cable 6 back
The following instructions are for a 6-stitch cable, but the same principal works for any size cable.

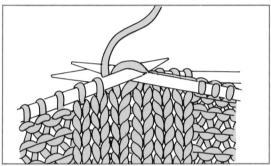

1 On the right side row, work to the position of the cable panel. Slip the next three stitches onto a cable needle and leave at the back of work. Knit the next three stitches in the usual way.

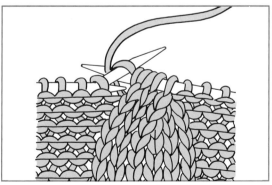

2 Now knit the three stitches from the cable needle, this completes the cable twist.

How to make a Cable 6 front

The following instructions are for a 6-stitch cable,
but the same principal works for any size cable.

1 On the right side row, work to the position of
the cable panel. Slip the next three stitches onto a
cable needle and leave at the front of work. Knit
the next three stitches in the usual way.

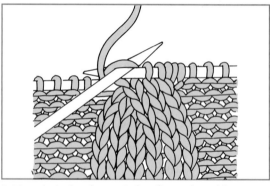

2 Now knit the three stitches from the cable
needle, this completes the cable twist.

Twisting stitches

Twisting stitches is the method used for altering the
direction of stitches to create a slanted, raised band.
It is most often used for moving knit stitches across
a reversed stocking stitch background. The slant
can be to the left or to the right depending on
whether the twist is worked at the back or the
front.

Most commonly only two stitches are moved at any
one time across one stitch every alternate row.

How to twist 2 back

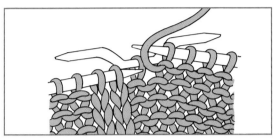

1 On a right side row purl to one stitch before the two stitches to be crossed. Slip the next stitch onto a cable needle and leave it at the back of the work.

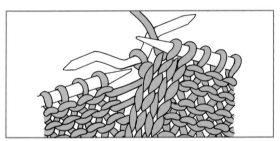

2 Knit the next two stitches on the lefthand needle.

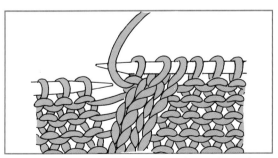

3 Now purl the stitch from the cable needle and continue to work in purl.

How to twist 2 front

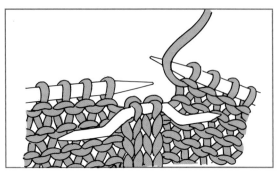

1 On a right side row purl to the two stitches to be crossed. Slip the next two stitches onto a cable needle and leave it at the front of the work.

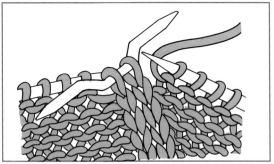

2 Purl the next stitch on the lefthand needle.

3 Now knit the two stitches from the cable needle, then continue to work in purl.

Bobbles

Bobbles are an important part of textured knitting, they can be used either as an all over pattern or in specific areas of a more complicated design.

The bobbles range in size from a small popcorn to a large bobble.

Methods vary slightly but the principle is always the same, a bobble is created by working extra stitches in one stitch, then working short rows on the extra stitches, before decreasing them back to the original stitch and continuing in pattern.

Bobbles can be worked in stocking stitch, reversed stocking stitch or garter stitch on any background stitch.

The following instructions are for one method of making a large bobble, with six stitches, in stocking stitch on a stocking stitch background.

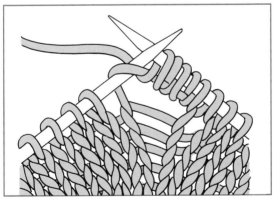

Row 1 Into the bobble stitch, work [yarn forward, knit 1] 3 times, thus making six stitches from one stitch. Turn the work.

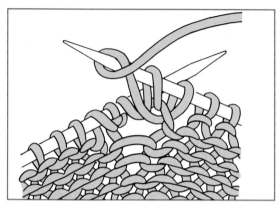

Row 2 (wrong side) Slip the first stitch, purl the remaining five stitches. Turn the work.

Row 3 Slip the first stitch, knit the remaining five stitches. Turn the work.

Row 4 [Purl 2 stitches together] 3 times. Turn the work.

Row 5 Slip the first stitch, knit the next two stitches together, pass the slipped stitch over the last stitch. This completes the bobble.

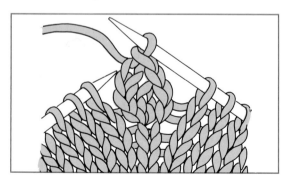

INTARSIA

This type of picture knitting involves working the different areas of colour in separate blocks without running the non-working colours along the row.

Twisting yarns together

When working intarsia, always twist the yarns on the wrong side of the work to avoid making a hole.

On a right side row, work to the colour change, then making sure both the yarns are at the back of the work, drop the first colour, pick up the second colour and bring it round the first colour to cross the yarns, before the working the next stitch.

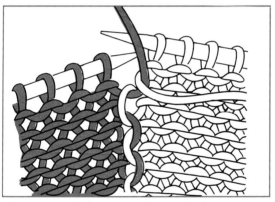

On a wrong side row, make sure both yarns are at the front of the work, drop the first colour, pick up the second colour and bring it round the first colour before working the next stitch.

This technique gives a neat unbroken line on the right side. Be sure to work the first stitch in each colour firmly to avoid a gap forming between the colour changes.

Diagonal slant to the right

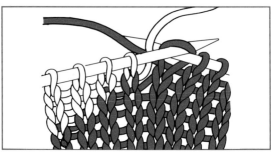

When the colour change slants to the right, the colours only have to be twisted on the right side rows. Take the first colour in front of the second colour, drop it, then pick up the second colour and work with it, thus twisting the colours. On the wrong side row the colours will automatically twist because of the direction of the slant.

Diagonal slant to the left

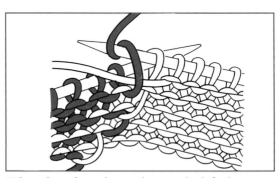

When the colour change slants to the left, the colours are twisted on the wrong side rows as shown. On the right side row the colours will automatically twist because of the direction of the slant.

Using bobbins

When using lots of colours in one row or the same colour in more than one area, it is easier to use small amounts of wool wound around bobbins. This stops the yarn from getting tangled and the work from becoming too heavy.

CIRCULAR KNITTING

Circular needles can be used for small seamless clothes such as berets and socks or for knitting yokes on jumpers and jackets. Jumper yokes are normally worked in rounds, but jacket yokes are worked on a circular needle in rows.

A yoke can be worked from the neck downwards, casting on at the neck and increasing outwards, changing to longer needles as the stitches are increased. The stitches are divided for back, front and sleeves, then the body and sleeves can be completed using circular and sets of double-pointed needles, leaving no sewing up to do.

There are many advantages to circular knitting: it is much quicker, since the knitting never has to be turned, and when working from a pattern the right side is always facing you, so you can see how the pattern is developing.

For Fair Isle patterns the yarn is always in the right place for the start of the round so there are fewer ends to neaten.

Using a circular needle

A circular needle has two pointed ends, joined by a strip of flexible nylon of varying lengths. Choose the correct length of needle, it is better to have too many stitches on a short needle than too few stitches on a long needle, which will stretch the knitting. If there is shaping involving a decrease in the number of stitches, you may have to change to a shorter needle.

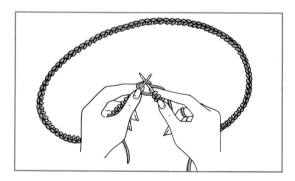

To start, cast on the number of stitches required, then spread them evenly along the complete length of the needle, making sure they are not twisted.

The first stitch of the first row is the stitch that was cast on first. To mark the beginning of the round, fold a short length of yarn, in a contrast colour, in half and make a slip knot, then slip the loop onto the needle at the beginning of the round.

On subsequent rounds, slip the loop from one needle to the next, so that you always know when you're starting and finishing a round.

Using a set of four needles

Using a set of needles is the best method for knitting a small number of stitches in rounds. Divide the number of stitches in three and cast this number of stitches onto each needle.

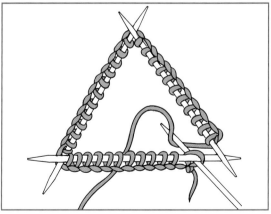

Making sure the stitches are not twisted, use the

fourth needle to knit the stitches from the first
needle, then use the free needle to knit the stitches
from the next needle. Continue in this way,
shaping as required.

Knitting flat circles and squares

Start by using five double-pointed needles. Cast 2
stitches onto each of four needles. Using the fifth
needle, work in rounds.

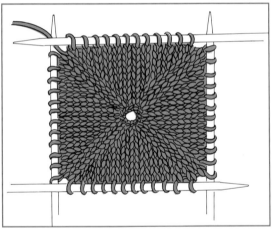

For a square, increase 1 stitch at each end of every
needle on every round, until the square is the size
required.

For a circle, increase 8 to 12 stitches evenly spaced
on alternate rounds.

For shapes with more than four sides, use a double-
pointed needle for each side plus an extra needle for
working with. Work as described for the square.

LACE KNITTING

Lace patterns can be used in many different ways - as an all over pattern, a horizontal or vertical panel or as motifs. They are most effective when worked in plain yarns as fluffy or textured yarns do not show the detail of the pattern. Fine yarns are more suitable than thick, as they give the fabric a more delicate look.

Lace stitch patterns are produced by increasing stitches and decreasing a corresponding amount of stitches, this may not necessarily be next to the increase or even on the same row.

A small pattern repeat is easy to follow, but a more complicated pattern over 24 or 32 rows should not be tackled by a beginner.

SWISS DARNING

This is a form of surface embroidery that duplicates the knitted stitches so that it looks as if the design has been knitted in. This technique is useful when working Fair Isle and Intarsia designs where small areas of colour can be Swiss darned rather than knitted in.

Always use the same thickness of yarn as for the background knitting.

Work from right to left. Thread a blunt ended needle with the embroidery yarn and weave in the yarn invisibly on the back of the work.

1 Bring the needle out at the base of the first stitch,

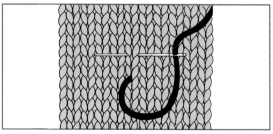

take it round the top of the stitch, under the stitch above.

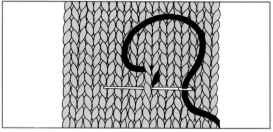

2 Insert the needle back through the base of the same stitch, thus covering the original stitch, bring the needle out at the base of the next stitch and continue in this way until the required area is covered.

BUTTONHOLES

A buttonhole is a small narrow slit worked in a border used for fastening a button. It needs to be worked neatly or it will stretch and become non-functional. The instructions in a pattern will state how many buttonholes to make and how far apart.

Eyelet buttonholes

These are the simplest buttonholes to make and are

suitable for fine yarns and baby clothes.

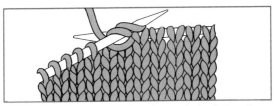

1 Knit to the position of the buttonhole, bring the yarn between the needles to the front of the work, then knit the next two stitches together.

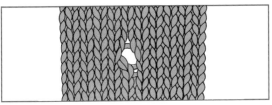

2 Work the next row normally to complete the buttonhole.

Vertical buttonholes

Use these for jackets in thick yarn where big buttons are required.

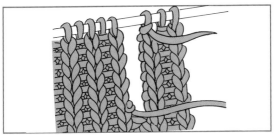

1 Work to the position of the buttonhole. Join in

another ball of yarn to the stitches on the lefthand
needle and continue to work each side separately
with their own balls of yarn.

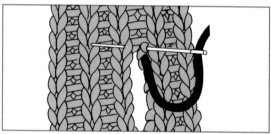

2 When the buttonhole is the required depth, close
the gap by working across both sets of stitches with
the first ball. Leaving a long end, cut off the second
ball. To complete the buttonhole, use the ends from
the second ball to strengthen the corners then darn
in the ends.

Horizontal buttonholes

These are worked over two rows and used on
cardigans and waistcoats.

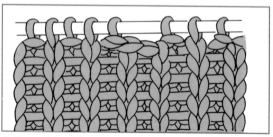

1 On a right side row, work to the position of the
start of the buttonhole, cast off, in pattern, the
required number of stitches, then work to the end
of the row.

2 On the next row, work to the cast-off stitches, turn the work and cast on the the same number of stitches using the cable method (see page 22), turn the work and complete the row.

HEMS

Hems are rarely used in knitting although stocking stitch hems can be used for jackets and coats. A picot edging is often used for baby clothes.

Sewn hem

The hem sections are knitted in stocking stitch on smaller needles than the main body of the garment and sewn in position when the garment is completed.

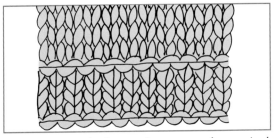

1 For a hem at the lower edge, cast on the required number of stitches. Starting with a knit row, work an odd number of rows in stocking stitch. Knit one more row to form the foldline. Change to the larger needles and, starting with a right side row, continue in pattern.

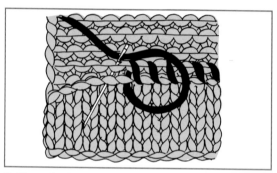

2 Turn the hem to the wrong side along the foldline and loosely sew the hem in place.

Knitted-in hem

The hem sections are knitted in stocking stitch on smaller needles than the main body of the garment and are knitted in before the garment is completed.

1 For a hem at the lower edge, cast on the required number of stitches. Starting with a knit row, work an odd number of rows in stocking stitch. Knit one

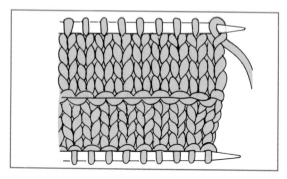

more row to form the foldline. Change to the larger needles and, starting with a right side row, continue in pattern for two rows less than the hem section. With a larger needle, purl one row. Using a spare needle, pick up one loop for each stitch along the cast-on edge.

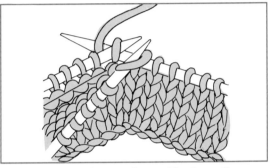

2 With wrong sides together and both needles facing in the same direction, *taking one stitch from each needle, knit both stitches together; rep from * to the end of the row, thus turning up the hem. Using correct needles, continue in pattern.

Picot hem

The hem sections are knitted in stocking stitch on smaller needles than the main body of the garment and are knitted in before the garment is completed. A row of eyelets is knitted at the level of the bottom of the hem, so that when the hem is turned up, they form a dainty edging. Suitable for fine yarns.

1 For a hem at the lower edge, cast on an odd number of stitches. Starting with a knit row, work an even number of rows in stocking stitch.

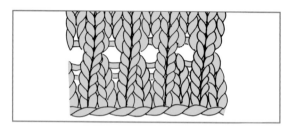

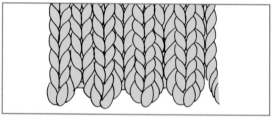

2 Now work the eyelet row as follows: K1, *yf, k2 tog; rep from * to end. Change to the larger needles and, starting with a wrong side row, continue in pattern for two rows less than the hem section. With a larger needle, purl one row. Using a spare needle, pick up one loop for each stitch along the cast-on edge. Complete as described for the sewn-in hem above.

Picot ridge

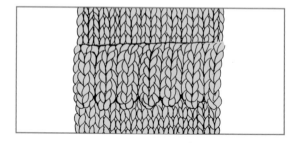

A picot ridge can be made anywhere on a piece of straight knitting by picking up the loops of a row instead of the cast-on edge.

Mock hem (invisible casting on)

This hem is used for ribbing. The bottom edge appears to have been neatly turned under, yet there is no double fabric and therefore no bulk. Use this technique where the ribbing is a main feature of the garment - for example, an all-over rib pattern or a fitted sweater with a deep welt.

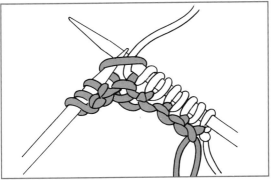

Using a contrast yarn of a similar weight, cast on half the total number of stitches required. Cut off the contrast yarn and join in the main yarn. Continue as follows:

Row 1 K1, ★yon (to make a st), k1; rep from ★ to end.

Row 2 K1, ★ytf, sl1 pw, ytb, k1; rep from ★ to end.

Row 3 Sl1 pw, ★ytb, k1, ytf, sl1 pw; rep from ★ to end.

Rows 4 and 5 As rows 2 and 3.

Continue in ordinary rib.

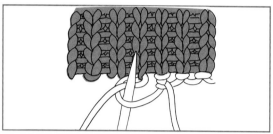

Unravel the contrast yarn.

SELVAGES
The side edges of a piece of knitted fabric are called selvages. Choose an edge that is suitable for the fabric and will give a neat edge.

Garter stitch fabric
Garter stitch fabric can be untidy at the beginning of the rows. To avoid this, work as follows:
1st row Slip the first stitch purlwise, take the yarn to the back between the needles, knit to the end of the row.

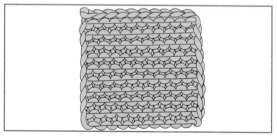

Repeat this row to produce a neat chain effect.
If the fabric is to be seamed, knit in the usual way without slipping the first stitch.

Stocking stitch fabric

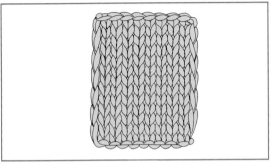

Simply slip the first stitch on every row, then proceed to the end of the row.

If the fabric is to be seamed, work as follows:

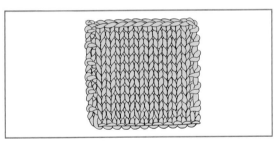

Row 1 Knit to end.
Row 2 K1, p to last st, k1.
Repeat these two rows to form a "pipped" edge, ideal for seaming.

POCKETS

Many garments feature pockets for both practical and decorative purposes. These fall into two categories - those which are knitted separately and sewn onto the knitting - called "patch pockets" - and those which are an integral part of the garment.

Precise instructions will be given in the working patterns. The following details give the common techniques.

Patch pockets

These are pockets which are knitted as a separate piece, then added to the right side of the garment.

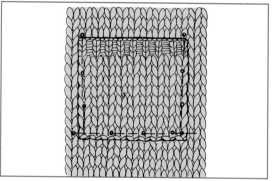

1 Pin the pocket in position on the background, lining the pocket up with the rows and the stitches.

2 Using a slip stitch, sew the pockets in place.

Horizontal pockets

A horizontal pocket is knitted into the garment as an integral part of the design.

1 Knit the pocket lining separately in stocking stitch, ending with a purl row. Cut off the yarn and slip the stitches onto a holder.

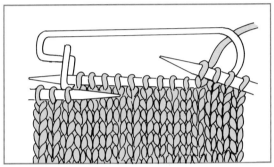

2 Work in pattern on the main part of the garment until you reach the pocket opening, ending on a wrong side row. **Next row** work to pocket position, then slip the group of stitches for the pocket front onto a holder.

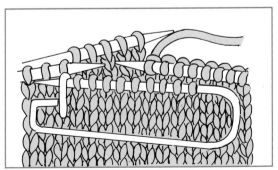

3 Work across the stitches of the pocket lining and work to the end of the row.

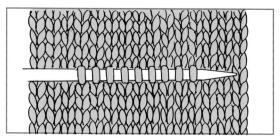

4 When the garment is completed, the stitches on the holder are worked in rib to neaten the top.

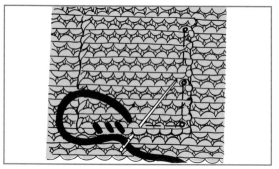

5 Pin the pocket lining in place on the wrong side and slip stitch in position around the sides and base.

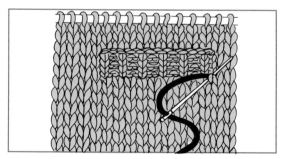

6 On the right side, sew down the sides of the ribbed pocket top.

Part 4:
CARE

CLEANING AND STORING

It is best to clean hand-knitted garments lightly and often, but with great care. Hand-knits are not as resilient as ready-made garments - they are more likely to stretch stretch out of shape or shrink if not handled carefully. Unless the ball band specifically states that the yarn can be machine washed, it is safest to hand wash or dry clean.

Hand washing

Use a special powder or solution for hand washing delicate fabrics. Completely dissolve the washing agent in warm water, then add sufficient cold water to make it lukewarm.

Immerse the garment in the suds and work quickly, using your hands to expel soapy water by gentle squeezing, never wringing.

Carefully lift the garment out of the water, support-ing it with both hands. Rinse the garment in clear water of the same temperature until the water runs clear. After rinsing, squeeze out as much water as possible, do not wring.

Drying

This needs as much care as washing. Supporting the weight of the garment, transfer the garment to a colourfast towel and lay it flat. Roll up the towel loosely so that excess moisture is transferred to the towel.

Natural fibres may be spun dry on a short gentle cycle and it is recommended that cotton is spun as the retained moisture may distort the garment.

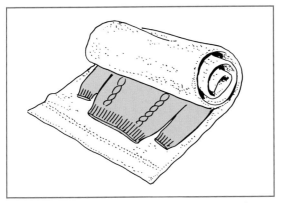

Lightly shake the garment to even out the stitches, lay it on the drying surface and gently reshape it back to its original size. Leave the garment until all the excess moisture has been absorbed by the towel. Leave to dry naturally.

Storage

Careful storage is as important as washing and drying. Never hang a knitted garment up, the weight of the garment pulls it out of shape and the ends of the hanger distorts the shapes of the shoulders.

Fold carefully. If the garment is to be stored for a long time interleave tissue paper in the garment when folding and place the garment in a plastic bag with plenty of holes in before storing.

REPAIRS AND ALTERATIONS

The most frequent problems due to wear or accidents on knitted garments are small holes and dropped stitches. Your most valuable asset is some

spare yarn – never throw any left-over yarn away –
even your tension square can be unravelled.

Holes

<u>Small</u>

Providing the hole is no deeper than one row and
the fabric is fairly plain, the edges can be grafted
together (see page 48). After undoing any damaged
stitches, use some spare yarn to graft the exposed
stitches and the join will be almost undetectable.

<u>Large</u>

The most difficult problem in the case of large holes
is the exposed sets of stitches, these can quickly
unravel. The hole can be repaired by grafting in a
knitted patch. First remove the damaged yarn by
carefully unpicking it to leave a neat hole with the
same number of exposed loops along the top as
there are at the bottom. Loosely knot the row-end
threads together to prevent further damage.

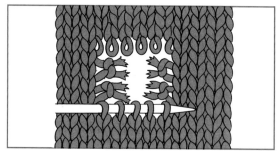

Using the loops from the lower edge of the hole
and the original needle size, work the same number
of rows that are missing. Finally, graft the last row

with the loops at the top of the hole. Sew down the side edges using an overcast seam. Secure the row-end threads as you are stitching.

Picking up a dropped stitch

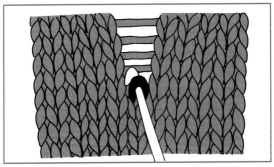

Insert a crochet hook into the dropped stitch from front to back. With the hook pointing up, catch the first horizontal strand of yarn from above and draw it through the dropped stitch. Continue in this way until the stitch is level with the row being worked, then replace it on the lefthand needle.

Picking up a row of stitches

The best way of picking up stitches if you have to undo more than a couple of rows is to remove the needle from the work and unravel the yarn to one row above the row to be undone. Work across the row slowly, gradually unpicking the stitches a few at a time and placing them on the needle. If some of the stitches are twisted, they can be untwisted as you knit the row by working into the back of the stitch.

Index